CUBANS

Sugarcane
Cuba's chief crop

IMMIGRATION AND THE AMERICAN WAY OF LIFE

Geologically speaking, the continent of North America is very old. The people who live here, by comparison, are new arrivals. Even the first settlers, the American Indians who came here from Asia about 35,000 years ago, are fairly new, not to speak of the first European settlers who came by ship or the refugees who flew in yesterday. Whenever they came, they were all immigrants. How all these immigrants live together today to form one society has been compared to the making of a mosaic. A mosaic is a picture formed from many different pieces. Thus, in America, many groups of people—from African Americans or Albanians to Tibetans or Welsh—live side by side. This human mosaic was put together by the immigrants themselves, with courage, hard work, and luck. Each group of immigrants has its own history and its own reasons for coming to America. Immigrants from different regions have their own way of creating communities for themselves and their children. In creating those communities, they not only keep elements of their own heritage alive, but also enrich further the fabric of American society. Each book in *Recent American Immigrants* will examine a part of this human mosaic up close. The books will look at some of the most recent arrivals to find out what they are like and how they fit into the whole mosaic.

Recent American Immigrants

CUBANS

Barbara Grenquist

Consultant
Roger Daniels, Department of History
University of Cincinnati

Franklin Watts

New York • London • Toronto • Sydney

Developed by: **Ω Visual Education Corporation**
Princeton, NJ

Maps: Patricia R. Isaacs/Parrot Graphics

Cover photograph: © Richard Haynes/RM International Photography

Photo Credits: p. 3 (L) David R. Frazier Photolibrary; p. 3 (M) Chuck
Fishman/Woodfin Camp & Associates, Inc.; p. 3 (R) Mark Downey; p. 9
H. Barnett/Peter Arnold, Inc.; p. 11 North Wind Picture Archives; p. 13
The University of Miami; p. 18 The University of Miami; p. 21 The
Langley Press; p. 22 The Miami Herald; p. 25 North Wind Picture
Archives; p. 30 Reuters/Bettmann; p. 32 Lee Lockwood/Black Star; p. 34
UPI/Bettmann Newsphotos; p. 35 UPI/Bettmann Newsphotos; p. 39
UPI/Bettmann Newsphotos; p. 40 Chuck Fishman/Woodfin Camp &
Associates, Inc.; p. 43 Olivier Rebbot/Woodfin Camp & Associates, Inc.;
p. 44 Tim Chapman/The Miami Herald; p. 46 Alon Reininger/Contact
Stock; p. 47 Courtesy of Carlos J. Arboleya; p. 49 Alon Reininger/
Contact Stock; p. 52 Al Diaz/The Miami Herald; p. 53 Alon Reininger/
Contact Stock; p. 55 Courtesy of Congresswoman Ileana Ros-Lehtinen;
p. 56 Michael Zagaris; courtesy of the Oakland Athletics; p. 58 The
Miami Herald; p. 61 The Miami Herald.

Library of Congress Cataloging-in-Publication Data

Grenquist, Barbara
Cubans / Barbara Grenquist.
p.   cm. — (Recent American immigrants)
Includes bibliographical references and index.
Summary: Describes how Cuban immigrants came to America to escape
repression in their homeland, and how they have adapted to life in the
United States while keeping their old traditions alive.
ISBN 0-531-11107-5
1. Cuban Americans—Juvenile literature.   2. United States—
Emigration and immigration—Juvenile literature.   3. Cuba—
Emigration and immigration—Juvenile literature.   [1. Cuban
Americans.   2. United States—Emigration and immigration.]
I. Title.   II. Series.
E184.C97G7   1991
305.868'7291073—dc20   90-12984 CIP AC

Contents

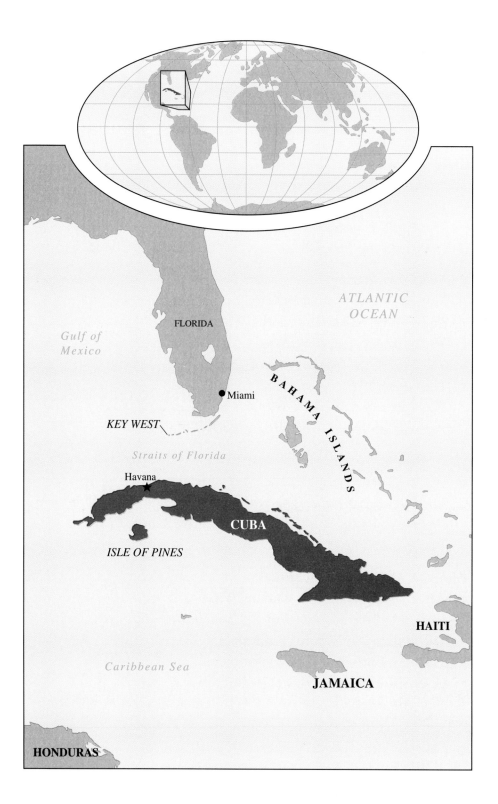

ATLANTIC
OCEAN

Gulf of
Mexico

FLORIDA

BAHAMA ISLANDS

● Miami

KEY WEST

Straits of Florida

Havana
★

CUBA

ISLE OF PINES

HAITI

Caribbean Sea

JAMAICA

HONDURAS

Early Cuba

Cuba is a beautiful island. Tall mountains and rolling hills cover about one-half of the land. The rest of the country is mostly gentle slopes and wide fields of grass. The coast is formed by deep bays, sandy beaches, and brightly colored reefs of coral.

Cuba is 745 miles long and 25 to 120 miles wide at different points. It is the largest island in the Caribbean Sea. Cuba is very close to the United States. It sits at the mouth of the Gulf of Mexico and is less than 100 miles from the islands at the end of Florida called the Keys. The capital city of Cuba is Havana. It is by far the largest and most important city in the country.

No part of Cuba is far from the sea. This makes the climate very mild, with breezes blowing over the land from the water to help cool even the hottest days. The temperature ranges from about seventy degrees in January to eighty-one degrees in July. There are two definite seasons: the "dry" season from November to April, and a hotter, "wet" season the rest of the time. The climate of Cuba is very much like the climate of Florida.

PLANT LIFE AND AGRICULTURE

Cuba has a rich plant life. There are more than 8,000 kinds of flowering plants on the island, which makes the landscape very fragrant and colorful. Much of the land has been planted with tropical crops, such as sugarcane, coffee, cacao, and bananas. Of these, sugarcane is by far the most important.

Sugar   Cuba has the kind of red soil that is perfect for growing sugarcane. There are cane crops planted all over the island. After the cane is harvested, it is milled to separate the juice from the stalk. The resulting liquid then goes through a process of clarification and crystallization into raw sugar and, finally, refined sugar and molasses.

The sale of sugar to the rest of the world has always been very important to Cuba. In fact, it is so important that a bad sugarcane crop in a given year can damage the economy of the whole country. As we will see later in the book, the United States stopped buying sugar from Cuba about thirty years ago. This has brought great hardship to Cuba ever since.

Other Industries   Other important agriculture industries in Cuba are the raising of dairy cattle and the growing of tobacco. Tobacco is a key crop, especially the kind of tobacco that is used to make cigars. The Cubans who make cigars are skilled craftsmen. The tobacco workers were among the first of the early Cubans to move to the United States and live in Florida. They were valued for their skill in rolling fine cigars. Cuban cigars are famous all over the world.

Cuba has a large mining industry, too. The Cubans mine copper, iron ore, nickel, and other minerals.

ANIMAL LIFE

There are many different kinds of animals on the island. Thirty kinds of bats live in Cuba. There are more bats than ground mammals on the island. Some bats live in abandoned buildings, but most of them make their homes in caves. The largest bat is big enough to catch fish; the smallest one is called the "butterfly bat."

Three kinds of large rats, including a rat that lives in trees, are found in forest and woodland areas. Alligators, iguanas, and several kinds of snakes are also to be found. There is one type of enormous boa constrictor—4.5 meters long (15 feet)—which eats pigs and goats, but it is not dangerous to humans. In the waters of some caves, where no light enters, the fish and shrimp are blind.

One of the strangest creatures in the Americas can be seen swimming at the mouths of rivers in Cuba: the manatee. The manatee has been nicknamed the "sea cow." Perhaps it got this nickname because it looks like a combination of a cow and a seal. Manatees can grow to be as long as 4.2 meters (14 feet).

Manatees, an endangered species, feed on sea grasses and have been overhunted for their meat, oil, and tough hide.

Columbus   Christopher Columbus touched shore on Cuba on his first voyage across the Atlantic Ocean. He was dazzled by the animal and plant life that he saw around him. He wrote a letter to Queen Isabella of Spain, who had paid for his journey, describing what he saw:

> *I have been so overwhelmed at the sight of so much beauty that I have not known how to relate it. The multitude of palm trees of various forms, the highest and most beautiful I have ever seen, and an infinity of other tall and green trees, the birds in rich plumage, and the verdure of the fields render this country . . . of such marvelous beauty that it surpasses all others in charms and graces as the day does the night in luster.*
>
> Source: As quoted in Nestor Carbonell, *And the Russians Stayed: The Sovietization of Cuba* (New York: Morrow, 1989), p. 13.

Columbus landed on Cuba on October 27, 1492. It was home to about 200,000 Indians. They were the Ciboney and Arawak tribes.

Columbus thought that Cuba was part of a continent, not an island. In 1508 Sebastian de Ocampo sailed around the island. Then it was clear that Columbus had been mistaken.

Conquest   The Spanish conquest of Cuba started in 1511. With a force of 300 armed men, it took Diego Velázquez less than two years to gain control of the island from the Indians.

Spain first used Cuba as a jumping-off point to explore the land that would be called America. Ships set sail in 1517 from the ports of Cuba and reached the part of Mexico called the Yucatán. Later Hernán Cortés departed from Cuba when he set off to conquer Mexico from 1519 to 1521. Hernando de Soto also left from Cuba when he headed north to explore Florida and the lower Mississippi valley.

Columbus preparing to go ashore on Cuba

Cuba soon became a supply and communications base for Spain. Havana became a very important Spanish port. Cuba was able to feed its own population and also provide food for the ships that sailed between the colonies and Spain. The main crops were fruits and vegetables. Cattle were also brought there and raised. Later, large plantations produced two important crops for export to the rest of the world: sugar and tobacco. Many workers were needed to tend and harvest these crops. The Spanish conquerors turned first to the Indians who lived on the island as a source of labor.

The Enslavement of the Indians The Indians of Cuba were skilled at agriculture. They also made pottery and highly polished stone tools. While one tribe might dominate the other, they were not warlike and lived together peacefully.

The Spanish brought a system of forced labor called *encomienda*. Having taken the Indians' land, the Spanish then demanded tribute from the Indians. In return, they offered "protection" and conversion to Christianity. When the Indians could not pay the tribute, they became slaves on their own land. They were also forced to work in the gold and silver mines. The Indians were overworked, beaten, and starved. Many of them died at the hands of the Spanish.

Many more died from disease. The Spanish had exposed the Indians to European illnesses as yet unknown in the New World. The Indians had no resistance to them, and by the middle of the sixteenth century, most of them had died. The Spanish, too, took home virulent New World diseases.

SLAVERY

With the disappearance of the Indians, there was a pressing need for laborers, especially on the sugar and tobacco plantations. Therefore, the Spanish decided to kidnap black people in Africa and bring them to the New World as slaves. Soon a large slave trade developed. From the middle of the sixteenth century until the slave trade ended in 1865, over 700,000 slaves

NORTH AMERICA

ATLANTIC OCEAN

Gulf of Mexico

Havana

CUBA

HISPANIOLA

Caribbean Sea

SOUTH AMERICA

PACIFIC OCEAN

SPANISH COLONIES
IN THE NEW WORLD
IN THE 1700s

Spanish Colonies

African slaves in Cuba

were brought to Cuba. By 1850, there were so many slaves in Cuba that the black people outnumbered the white.

Many of the slave owners treated the slaves brutally. The plantation owners feared that the slaves might rise up in a successful revolution against the cruelty of their masters, as the slaves in nearby Haiti had accomplished in 1804. So when a slave revolt threatened in Cuba in 1812, the Spanish quickly crushed it. They hanged Antonio Aponte, the leader of the revolt, and all of his followers.

While life was harsh for the slaves, the Spanish slave laws also made it possible for a slave to purchase his own freedom. Many of the slaves who did not die of beatings and overwork took advantage of this opportunity to become Cuban citizens. Although the slave trade ended in 1865, slavery was not finally abolished until 1886.

CUBA AND THE SPANISH EMPIRE

Throughout the seventeenth and eighteenth centuries, Cuba was at the mercy of Spain. Cuba was allowed to trade only with the mother country, and all Cuban goods had to be carried on Spanish ships. Control of the military and the economy on the island was in the hands of the Spanish-born *peninsulares* (people from the peninsula of Spain), not the native-born Cubans of Spanish descent, the *creoles*. And the creoles were bitter about the discrimination.

Cuba suffered great destruction and loss of life when the island became the target of attacks from rival European countries, who were also trying to get a foothold in the Caribbean. Natural disasters, such as hurricanes and epidemics, took their toll, too. Events reached a low point when the English occupied Havana for ten months in 1762.

Cuba began to prosper again in the late 1700s. Trade was opened with the newly independent United States. By 1791, the population of Cuba was about 172,000.

Desire for Independence   In spite of economic progress, the Cubans still rankled from old hardships. They were discontented and restless. Spain's failure to grant self-government and its imposition of increased taxes sparked revolts in Cuba. Beginning with Mexico in 1809, almost all of Spain's New World possessions broke away and became independent. By the mid-nineteenth century only Puerto Rico and Cuba remained of the vast empire Columbus and his successors gave Spain. In 1868, the first war for Cuban independence broke out. It was called the Ten Years' War.

THE TEN YEARS' WAR

The rebellion's leader was a rich planter and lawyer named Carlos Manuel de Céspedes. Under the banner of revolution, he called for independence for Cuba and an end to slavery.

The Bitter War   The war was fought fiercely on both sides. An estimated 200,000 Spaniards and 50,000 Cubans were killed. Many Americans wanted to come to the aid of the Cubans, but the U.S. government remained neutral. Thirty years would go by before the United States would take an active role in the fight for Cuban independence.

The Ten Years' War ended in 1878, when Spain agreed to the Pact of Zanjón.

The Pact of Zanjón, 1878

Article 1.   Concession to the Island of Cuba of the same political privileges, organic and administrative, as those enjoyed in the Island of Puerto Rico. [Two years earlier Puerto Rico had been granted representation in the Spanish parliament.]

Article 2.   Amnesty for political offenses between 1868 and 1878, and freedom to those indicted, or under sentence, either within or out of the island; a general pardon to the deserters from the Spanish army without distinction of nativity, making this clause extensive to all those who may have taken part, directly or indirectly, in the revolutionary movement.

Article 3.   Freedom to the slaves and Chinese who are today in the insurgent ranks.

[Further clauses concerned military service, the right to leave the island, and details about the laying down of arms.]

The Different Races in Cuba

Today, the Cuban population is made up of three racial groups: African, European, and Asian.

Blacks Most Cuban blacks today are descended from African slaves brought there. Others came from Jamaica and Haiti to work as field hands during harvest time and stayed on. People from different racial groups have also married one another. One of Cuba's most powerful twentieth-century leaders, Fulgencio Batista, was descended from all three racial groups. We will discuss him later in the book.

Whites Most of the white people in Cuba are descended from the Spaniards. But people from other European countries also live there. Cuba accepted many immigrants who had lost their homes during World War II. More recently, Cuba has had close relations with the Soviet Union and its allies, such as Poland and Czechoslovakia. People from these countries have also come to Cuba to work and to live.

Chinese Many Chinese were imported as indentured servants to take the place of the black slaves when the slave trade ended in 1865. Indentured servants agreed to work for someone for a set period of time—usually eight years. In return, they received their boat fare to Cuba, food, and lodging. The Chinese worked very hard and eventually found a secure place in the Cuban economy. When they had worked off their servitude, they became owners of laundries, restaurants, and other small businesses. They made up a small but important percentage of the population.

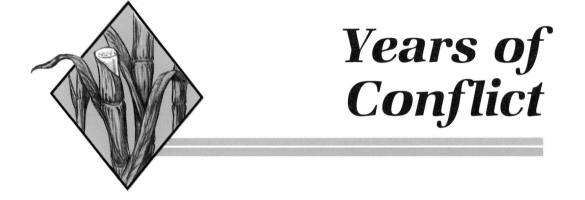

Years of Conflict

One of the earliest Cubans to come to the United States was a Catholic priest, Father Félix Varela (1788–1853). Born in Havana, Varela studied at the College and Seminary of San Carlos there. He entered the priesthood and became a distinguished teacher. He was an early believer in educational reform and a backer of the brief constitutional government established in Spain in 1812. Sent to Spain in 1822, he worked in the liberal parliament to bring about self-government in Cuba and other colonies.

With the return of the repressive monarchy of Ferdinand VII, Varela fled to New York late in 1823 and served at various churches. In 1835, he became rector of the Church of the Transfiguration. It became an important religious center, especially for Irish Americans. There were hardly any other Cubans in the city.

Father Varela played an active role in the lives of the people of his parish. He established schools and nurseries, and ministered to the ill during a cholera epidemic. He retired to St. Augustine, Florida, in 1851, and died there two years later. He received many honors after his death.

The most important first settlements of Cubans in the United States were in Key West and Tampa, Florida. In the 1830s, about fifty Cubans lived in Key West. Later, when action in the Ten Years' War caused many of the Cuban tobacco fields to be burned, people lost their jobs. Cigar makers like Vincente Martínez Ibor and Eduardo Hidalgo Gato moved their factories to Key West or Tampa. They took with them a large number of skilled workers.

The first Cuban cigar makers went to Tampa in 1866 on a side-wheeler steamboat. They found conditions of work good in large factories with high windows. The windows were left open to let in fresh air and light. The cigar makers needed bright light to roll the tobacco leaves.

The cigar makers brought with them a custom known previously not only in Cuba but also all over the international cigar-making world: reading by a *lector*. The lector's job was to read to the workers all day long as they bent over the long factory tables, forming the cigars. Readers sat on a raised platform or chair at the front of the large workrooms. They read a great variety of texts—newspapers, political tracts, and works of literature. Among the workers' favorite books were the classic seventeenth-century Spanish novel *Don Quixote*, by Miguel de Cervantes, and *The Three Musketeers*, the nineteenth-century novel by the French writer Alexandre Dumas.

The lector was highly respected. One Cuban American remembers:

> *Each evening my sister would come home and give us verbally what had happened. We stuck around the family table some thirty minutes or so after supper to hear my sister give us the episode of the day . . . she had heard from the lector.*

Early Cuban cigar makers in Florida

A retired cigar worker recalls:

> *Sometimes he [the lector] read a novel, he read so good that people stand . . . stand and look at him.*
>
> Source: Both of the above quotes appear in Margaret S. Boone, *Capital Cubans: Refugee Adaptation in Washington, D.C.* (New York: AMS Press, 1989), p. 164.

Descendants of the first Cuban families who came to live in Tampa still live in the Ybor City section of the city.

José Martí (1853–1895)

José Martí was one of Cuba's great revolutionary heroes. A fighter for Cuban independence all his life, Martí was also an outstanding political and literary writer. To this day, he is a symbol of liberty throughout Latin America.

As a young man, Martí sided with the Cuban independence fighters during the Ten Years' War. He was arrested by the government and sent to prison to work at hard labor for six months. In 1871 he was deported to Spain. He returned to Cuba in 1878 and took up his political activities once more. Again he was deported to Spain. He spent brief periods in France, Mexico, and Venezuela, and finally settled in the United States.

Martí moved to New York in 1881, where he was elected head of the Cuban revolutionary party and brought together Cuban exile groups. He visited Florida many times to gain the support of Cuban cigar makers for independence. In New York he also gained worldwide fame as a literary figure. He wrote for several Latin American newspapers and crafted poems, plays, and novels. Although he was on the side of the poor and oppressed, Martí did not advocate socialism. At the same time, he was often critical of U.S. policies.

On April 11, 1895, José Martí led an invasion of Cuba. He was killed in battle a month later. Cuban independence was yet to be won.

THE CUBAN WAR FOR INDEPENDENCE

The Ten Years' War had ended on a high note for Cuba. Peace did not last long, however. Spain told the Cubans that they would have to pay for property that had been damaged during the war. Spain also did not carry out the political reforms it had promised. In 1895, the Cubans rose up again.

The revolt was caused not only by Spanish misrule but by U.S. tariff policy. In 1894, high duties were levied on raw sugar. This meant Americans stopped buying so much sugar from abroad. Because most of Cuba's principal export crop of sugar went to the United States, Cuban sugar plantations and mills all but shut down. Thousands of workers lost their jobs.

The last straw came when Spain took away some of the rights guaranteed to Cubans under the constitution. At this point José Martí led his band of rebels back to Cuba.

THE UNITED STATES ENTERS THE WAR

Spain sent more than 200,000 troops to Cuba to fight the rebels. The revolutionaries fought back with a so-called scorched-earth policy. They burned everything in their path, including the plantations. They did this in the hope that Spain would give up fighting if there was nothing on the island worth fighting for.

The Spanish set up detention camps for the civilian population. Men, women, and children were herded together in unspeakable conditions, often with no protection from the elements. Many people died of hunger and disease.

The United States protested against the treatment of innocent civilians. To the American public, Spain seemed ruthless and cruel. By now, American public opinion supported the Cubans.

Remember the Maine!   The U.S. battleship *Maine* blew up in Havana harbor in 1898. Today, scholars are almost certain the explosion was an accident. But at the time, many Americans thought the Spanish had sunk the ship and were responsible for the loss of 260 of its crew. "Remember the *Maine!*" became the popular battle cry for revenge. And the United States declared war on Spain.

THE SPANISH-AMERICAN WAR

The war was over in a few months. This was owing more to Spanish weakness and disorganization than to American strength. The United States did have a very much more powerful navy and was able to sink most of the Spanish fleet. Finally Spain signed a treaty promising to give up all claims to Cuba.

Theodore Roosevelt   Theodore Roosevelt, later president of the United States, became a popular hero of the Spanish-American War when he led a regiment of American cavalry called the "Rough Riders" into battle. This ragtag group of men, which included everyone from millionaires to cowboys, played a big role in capturing San Juan Hill. This victory both weakened Spanish morale and helped launch Roosevelt as a national figure.

Actually, the American army had been poorly prepared for war and poorly supplied once in it. Only a few hundred soldiers and sailors died in battle, whereas over 5,000 died of dysentery, malaria, and other diseases.

THE FIRST U.S. OCCUPATION OF CUBA

The Spanish domination of Cuba came to an end on January 1, 1899. United States military forces remained in Cuba until 1902. During this time, the Americans helped bring improve-

Colonel Theodore Roosevelt in 1898

ments in public works, sanitation, and education. In doing so, they laid the groundwork for years of domination of the island by the United States.

The Platt Amendment   In 1901, Congress passed the Platt Amendment, which spelled out relations between the United States and Cuba. Cuba was pressured to incorporate the document in its constitution. The Platt Amendment stated that the United States could send troops to preserve Cuba's independence and could intervene anytime to make sure there was "protection of life, property, and individual liberty." Finally, Cuba had to sell or lease lands to the United States for naval bases. And in 1903, the United States established a naval base at Guantánamo Bay. It is still in operation.

THE SECOND U.S. OCCUPATION OF CUBA

The Cubans took over the government from the U.S. military occupation forces on May 20, 1902. The first president of the new republic was Tomás Estrada Palma. At the beginning, his government seemed to be doing well. But Estrada used dishonest means to get reelected in 1906. The result was revolution, and Estrada asked the United States to intervene again, to many Cubans' displeasure.

A provisional government lasted until 1909, when the Cuban republic was declared for the second time. A series of governments followed thereafter, ending with the regime of Fulgencio Batista, who took the reins of power in 1933.

Walter Reed and Yellow Fever

While revolution and war were at their height in the Caribbean, an important medical discovery was made. Yellow fever was a disease the Cubans (and many other peoples around the world) had suffered from for a long time. No one knew the cause of it for sure. During the Spanish-American War, an epidemic of yellow fever broke out among the American soldiers. Walter Reed, a doctor in the army, was made the head of a committee to investigate the disease marked by high fever, nausea, jaundice, and often death.

At the time, the disease was considered contagious, that is, transmitted by contact with someone who was sick with the disease. But the Cuban Carlos Juan Finlay had already thought that a certain mosquito carried the disease. Reed put Finlay's theory to the test in 1900. Usually medical experiments are done on animals. But Reed couldn't use animals because animals did not catch yellow fever. He used human volunteers to show that the disease was not transmitted from one person to another but by mosquito bites. This resulted in the introduction of a vaccine and a worldwide attempt to control the mosquito population.

From 1902 on, Cuba grew more and more economically dependent upon the United States. These were years of unrest and instability. Well-meaning governments were incompetent, and there were corrupt governments as well. There was prosperity during World War I. During the twenties and the thirties, U.S. financial interests in Cuba grew. North Americans came to own a large share of Cuban industry in sugar, oil, agriculture, banking, transportation, tourism, and gambling.

General Gerardo Machado was first elected president in 1924. His was a rule of terror. At the same time, the economy slumped. The price of sugar dropped, and in 1933 the army ousted him from office.

The Good Neighbor Policy   In his first inaugural in 1933, President Franklin D. Roosevelt pledged the United States to the "policy of the good neighbor." At a conference of Latin American nations, Secretary of State Cordell Hull supported the declaration that "no state has the right to intervene in the internal or external affairs of another." Roosevelt declared that the United States was opposed to armed intervention.

The United States promised to cooperate with its neighbors in the Western Hemisphere, including Cuba, where so many Americans owned property. As World War II drew near, Roosevelt urged friendship between North and South American nations—especially in terms of collective security and mutual defense agreements.

Batista Takes Over   Fulgencio Batista was only a sergeant in the Cuban army at the time Machado left office. But through his connections and his dynamic personality, he soon gained control of the army. He also gained the power behind the government for two decades, though he usually remained discreetly in the wings. He had the support of the U.S. government as well. Even though the North Americans might disapprove of his power, they approved of his protection and support for U.S. business interests in Cuba. He backed a new constitution in 1940. He became president in that year, and he remained in office until 1944.

WORLD WAR II

Cuba declared itself an ally of the United States on the day after the Japanese bombed Pearl Harbor in 1941, as did many other Latin American nations. The Cuban foreign minister declared that Cuba looked upon the attack "as an attack against Cuba." These were prosperous years for the planters, and the Cubans kept their ships loaded with sugar coming to the United States. They were also dangerous years, for German submarines were on the prowl for merchant ships carrying raw materials to the United States. During the war, Cuba lost at least three ships to submarine attacks.

POSTWAR BATISTA

Domestic life was still in turmoil in Cuba, though hope ran high for free and democratic elections following the war. Batista brought these hopes to an end by forcibly taking over the government when it became clear in the 1952 elections that he would not win. For a time, Batista seemed all-powerful. He enjoyed the support of the United States. He condoned graft and corruption. He manipulated elections. He arranged the murder of 20,000 people who had opposed him. He jailed many more. The various Cuban political parties could not get together to form a broad coalition to oust him from power, either by negotiation or force. Opposition ranging from the Communist Party to the Catholic church were ineffective in bringing about his downfall. The country had had enough. It searched desperately for a solution and would find it in yet another revolution.

BACKGROUND TO REVOLUTION

Historical Causes   As we have seen, throughout its history Cuba was dominated by a foreign power. When it finally revolted against Spain and became independent at the end of the nineteenth century, Cuba simply exchanged one power for another. The United States soon became a large trade and financing partner in the Cuban economy. For some years, it also took a leading role in Cuba's internal and foreign affairs and established a large naval base on Cuban territory. While many Cubans prospered—most were poor—Cuba floundered politically from several governments that existed only through military force, graft, and corruption.

Recent Causes   By the 1950s, the Batista government was reaping a final harvest of bloodshed and corruption from a socially and politically ill society. There were longtime and deep racial and social divisions among the Cuban people, few of whom, except politicians and their families, saw any of the returns from the prosperous Cuban economy. Most of the wealth was in the hands of a tiny percentage of the population. Nearly 50 percent of the farmland was held by about 1 percent of the landowners. The rural population (about 40 percent of the total) did not fare as well as those people who lived in the cities. Peasant farmers earned only about 10 percent of the country's income. Health care was generally good, although harder to come by in the country than in the cities. Corruption and influence also affected health care, as well as other spheres of life in Cuba.

The Cuban Revolution: 1959 and After

Fidel Castro was born in 1926 near Birán, in Oriente province at the eastern end of Cuba. His father had been born in Spain and was a farmer of comfortable means. His mother was a Cuban.

As a boy, Castro already showed signs of leadership and rebellion. He had a difficult relationship with his father and had constant brawls with other children. Combative by nature, he was also a good athlete. He was strong and seemingly fearless and took on all competitors. A good student, especially in history, Castro—like many Cubans—worshiped José Martí and set him up as a model all his life. As a teenager, reportedly he decided at one point that his father was not treating his workers fairly. To his father's dismay and anger, Castro advised the workers to go on strike. His mother was more understanding and admired Castro's spirit.

Castro attended Roman Catholic boarding schools in Santiago and Havana and obtained a doctorate in law in 1950 from the University of Havana.

While at the university, Castro joined in student political activities. He was elected a delegate to the Student Federation and participated in the organized violence of action groups or gangs involved in national politics. More and more idealistic, Castro joined a new party called *Ortodoxos,* which stood for nationalism, anti-imperialism, and social justice, among other things. In 1947, he joined a group of Cubans and Dominican exiles in an unsuccessful expedition to overthrow Rafael Trujillo, dictator of the Dominican Republic. In 1948, he participated in student riots in Bogotá, Colombia, at the Ninth Inter-American Conference.

A young and beardless Castro at a political demonstration in Havana in 1952

Though he would not declare himself a Communist until later, Castro had worked with Communist as well as Catholic revolutionary students. He probably also began to read Communist literature during his student years.

EARLY REVOLUTIONARY LEADER

Following Batista's power grab in 1952, Castro emerged as a young student revolutionary leader of the forces against Batista. With a band of fewer than 200 rebels, he led a disastrous attack against the military base in Moncada on July 26, 1953. Most of the group were killed, and Castro and his younger brother Raul, who had also participated, were sent to prison.

Challenge to History   When Castro went on trial, he attacked the corrupt and repressive policies in his self-defense. He used the name of José Martí. He called for the redistribution of land and wealth and the restoration of democracy and justice in Cuba. "Sentence me," he declared, "but history will absolve me."

THE REVOLUTION BEGINS

After he was released from prison in 1955, Castro went to Mexico to train rebels to attack Batista. They called their revolutionary forces, known as "guerrillas," the "26th of July Movement" in memory of the Moncada attack. In December 1956, a band of guerrillas landed in Cuba from aboard the yacht *Granma*. They were immediately attacked and overcome on the beach by Batista forces. Almost all were killed. Castro and a few others, including Raul Castro and the Argentinian revolutionary Ernesto (Che) Guevara, retreated into the mountains known as Sierra Maestra in Oriente province. Batista decided not to pursue Castro into this barren and remote area.

A rare photo of Castro (center) and his top command in the revolutionary forces at a secret base in the Sierra Maestra in 1957. Raul Castro, Fidel's brother, kneels in foreground. Ernesto (Che) Guevara, official physician of the rebel army, is second from left.

The Robin Hood of the Sierra Maestra   In fact, Batista claimed that Castro was dead. And when the *New York Times* published an interview with the very much alive Castro early in 1957, Batista, proven wrong, began to lose his backing, both at home and among some Americans. While he tried to find Castro's forces in the mountains and surrounded the area, he let loose a reign of terror in the cities.

Support and supplies for Castro and his rebels, by then almost folk heroes, poured in from Latin America and from supporters in the United States. Their guerrilla activity in the mountains caught the imagination of the world, and newspaper and television stories compared Castro to José Martí. The *New York Times* called him "the Robin Hood of the Sierra Maestra."

In March 1958 the United States banned the shipping of any more arms to the government in Havana. Batista, however, would continue to use airplanes supplied by the United States for some months against the rebels. Casualties were heavy among civilians, and Castro, blaming the United States, would never forget this. In April, Castro called for a general strike throughout Cuba, but it was a failure. Batista took heart because of it and ordered offensive action against the rebels that lasted seventy-six days. The rebels, now confident and practiced, repeatedly won their skirmishes against government troops. By August the Batista forces were demoralized.

By the end of October, the rebels had broken out of the Sierra Maestra and were fighting throughout the country. Government military units began to defect, and in spite of a last stand by Batista, it was clear that his government would not remain in power for long.

Despite pressure from the United States, as well as from his own military, Batista hung on. This allowed Castro to make further and further gains. Finally, on New Year's Day, 1959, Batista fled the country, and the rebel forces took over.

Fulgencio Batista, before fleeing Cuba

THE NEW GOVERNMENT

Manuel Urrutia, a former judge and political moderate, became president, and Castro took over as premier. Castro said he would restore the constitution of 1940, which stated that the president had to be forty years old. Castro was only thirty-two. He constantly roamed Havana, talking with his compatriots and basking in their adulation.

One of his first duties, as he saw it, was to bring to justice those responsible for killings and torture under Batista. Many Cubans were in favor of vengeance, and Castro responded by conducting mass trials, sometimes in stadiums, which were later followed by executions. Foreign reaction, especially in the United States, was critical, and some of the favorable opinion about the revolution began to melt away.

In his speeches, which were often hours long, yet spellbinding to his supporters, Castro repeatedly said that he was not seeking the presidency and that the revolution was not Communist. He was, however, de facto leader of the country, making all the important decisions. No elections were called, and meetings of his cabinet, or advisers, became less frequent.

CASTRO VISITS THE UNITED STATES

In April 1959 Castro traveled to the United States at the invitation of the Society of Newspaper Editors. Crowds were large wherever he went, and he spoke to many people about his aims to bring democracy and better economic conditions to his people. Following a meeting with Castro, Vice President Richard Nixon told the State Department that the Cuban leader represented a threat to the interests of the United States. Nixon also said that Castro was being influenced by Communists. The United States recognized the new Cuban government but denied it financial and political support.

Castro had always thought land reform was key to bringing about social and economic change in Cuba. An agrarian law was passed in May 1959 limiting ownership of land to 1,000 acres. Exceptions were made for especially productive Cuban sugar and rice plantations and foreign companies, if these holdings were considered in the national interest. The rest of the acreage would be taken over and turned into cooperatives or given in small amounts to sharecroppers.

Consolidation   Castro, carefully playing off one political faction against another in Cuba, was moving closer to communism. A colorful meeting with Soviet premier Nikita Khrushchev took place at the United Nations in New York. Concerned about the radical turn of Castro's revolution and about his growing ties with the Soviet Union, the United States cut back the amount of sugar it would buy from Cuba. In response, Castro took over more than $1 billion of U.S. property, including land, banks, and oil companies, as well as property of other foreign countries. Relations with the United States became strained. Khrushchev offered to buy a large amount of Cuban sugar and also offered support and arms to Cuba in the event of a confrontation with the United States. Early in 1961, the Eisenhower administration in Washington broke diplomatic ties with Cuba when Castro demanded a drastic cut in the U.S. embassy staff in Havana.

Cubans Leave the Country   As the extent of Castro's revolution became clear, Cuban business owners and middle-class professionals, many trained in the United States, had to make a decision whether to support Castro or not. Many decided it was not in their best interests to stay. Thus began what would become a large exodus of people from Cuba to the United States.

THE BAY OF PIGS

Newly elected U.S. president John F. Kennedy took office on January 20, 1961. He soon approved a plan for the invasion of Cuba that had originated in the Eisenhower administration. The invasion force was to consist of exile Cubans, trained by U.S. agencies and others in Guatemala. No American forces would take part. On April 14, an air strike from Nicaragua failed to do much damage to Castro's air force. On April 17, an expedition of about 1,300 troops landed at two beaches, Playa Girón and Playa Larga, in Bahía de Cochinos (the Bay of Pigs), 110 miles southeast of Havana. The invasion was a fiasco. It was poorly planned, the exiles were not well trained, and the hoped-for military support by the Cuban underground failed to appear. Exile casualties were estimated to be between 85 and 150, and the rest of the troops were taken prisoner. They were taken to Havana, and some were publicly interrogated by Castro. Eventually Castro asked for and received a ransom of $53 million in medical and food supplies, and the prisoners were released. Instead of hurting Castro, the invasion resulted in an upsurge of popularity for him and a wave of propaganda condemning "imperialist aggression."

Castro Declares He Is Communist   At the end of 1961, Castro declared that he was a Marxist-Leninist. Early in 1962, the Organization of American States (OAS) voted to exclude Cuba. Beset with economic problems at home, Castro tried to strengthen his ties with the Soviet Union. Khrushchev, looking for more friendly relations with the United States, kept a cautious stance in regard to Cuba for the time being.

BACKGROUND OF THE COLD WAR

Momentous as the events in Cuba were, they were happening within the larger framework of a much more dangerous world situation, the so-called cold war. It had started soon after the end of World War II, when Communist Soviet Union took over many countries in Eastern Europe. The cold war described the nonmilitary struggle taking place between the United States and the Soviet Union for influence and power in the world. It was a dangerous struggle because of the threat of the use of nuclear weapons. Previous crises in Europe had already provided for a tense international atmosphere.

Then in October 1962, U.S. intelligence produced evidence that the Soviets were building missile sites in Cuba. Khrushchev denied it, but the American ambassador to the United Nations produced photographs taken by U.S. reconnaissance planes for all the world to see. President Kennedy considered it an act of aggression by the Soviet Union. He placed a naval and air blockade around Cuba against the delivery of the weapons. Soviet ships headed for Cuba stopped, but work on the missile sites continued. The world held its breath as the United States prepared for an air attack on the island. Finally, Khrushchev agreed to remove the missiles in exchange for an American promise not to invade Cuba. The most dangerous confrontation between superpowers since World War II had come to a peaceful end.

Both countries, in effect, had made a choice against nuclear war. It again seemed possible to hope for peace. And the following summer, the two countries took a first step toward an arms agreement by banning the testing of nuclear weapons in the atmosphere.

Adlai Stevenson, U.S. ambassador to the United Nations, speaks out strongly against the building of Soviet missile sites in Cuba in 1962.

The New Cuban Americans

Following Castro's takeover in 1959, some people connected with the ousted Batista government came to the United States. However, the 1960 U.S. census counted a total of only about 124,000 Cuban Americans, most of whom had been in the country for years. Large numbers of Cubans began to come during 1960 as it became clear that Cuban society was going to be completely reorganized. Though diplomatic relations between the United States and Cuba ceased in January 1961, the airlines continued to carry passengers from Havana until the missile crisis in October 1962. Most direct communication between the two countries stopped at that time.

From 1959 to 1962, more than 200,000 Cubans came to the United States. They were given refugee status, which meant that they could get financial and other support from the federal government. Exiles in the first wave were for the most part well educated and wealthy, although many had to leave most of their property in Cuba. Castro would let people go, but not assets. As indicated earlier, they made up a large portion of the business and professional middle class in Cuba.

AFTER 1962

For the three years following 1962, when air travel from Cuba was not available, immigration from Cuba dropped to a total of about 9,000. Cubans wishing to leave their country had to depart in secrecy by any means they could, often on small boats. Others arranged to fly first to a third country, most often Mexico or Spain, from where they could then enter the United States.

Then in 1965, President Lyndon Johnson made a special agreement with Cuba that established an airlift between Cuba and Miami, Florida. Flights took off daily and over the next eight years brought some 368,000 Cubans to the United States. The airlift ended in 1973, and immigration has tapered off greatly. Since 1973, most Cubans wishing to come to the United States now must be able to travel to another country first.

WHO THE CUBANS WERE

Not all the Cubans who came were wealthy bankers, landowners, or government officials, although the number of professionals, such as physicians, who came caused a serious shortage in Cuba for a while. Some people at all levels of the Cuban society had not liked the changes Castro was bringing to their country and left. Before the airlift ended, it had brought a large number of lower-middle-class and blue-collar workers. However, the largest number of people in the Cuban American population are middle class and white. Blacks from Cuba were slow to come. Not only were most of them poor, but also they were aware of the often harsh racism in the United States. Peasant farmers are almost not represented at all. Many of the small Chinese Cuban community also came, as did eventually a large proportion of the elderly in the population.

The last mass exodus from Cuba occurred in 1980. A number of Cubans who wanted to leave sought asylum in the unguarded Peruvian embassy in Havana. Castro said anyone who wanted to could leave from the nearby port of Mariel. He was surprised, however, by the number of people who chose to go. As the word spread that people could leave for America, the crowd grew. A fleet of small boats organized by exiles in Miami picked up over 130,000 "Marielitos," most of them working people. Reception centers in Florida became overburdened, and a stop to the flow of people finally had to be negotiated.

A boat full of Marielitos on its way to Miami in 1980

For some Marielitos, the journey to the United States meant separation from loved ones. This family had to leave Cuba without husband and father.

U.S. REFUGEE POLICY

In 1959, President Dwight Eisenhower allocated $1 million to help Cubans settle in the United States. This money was to be used to meet emergency needs, such as housing, food, and clothing. Continuing through presidents Kennedy, Johnson, Nixon, and Carter, and through the time of the Mariel boat lift, a total of $1.4 billion has been spent on aiding the Cuban refugees.

As defined in the Refugee Assistance Act of 1980, a refugee is a person who is unable or unwilling to return to his or her own country "because of persecution or a well-founded fear of persecution on account of race, religion, nationality, membership in a particular social group, or political opinion."

U.S. policy has generally allowed people wishing to enter the United States from countries considered hostile to U.S. interests (that is, Communist countries) to be classified as refugees. Thus Cubans have had a distinct advantage over some other Caribbean and Central American peoples, such as Salvadorans and Haitians, who flee from brutal regimes that are not Communist. The U.S. government has maintained that these latter are considered economic refugees and thus are not eligible for refugee status.

THE CUBAN AMERICAN COMMUNITY

Since 1959, more than 700,000 Cubans have settled in the United States. Cuban Americans now live in every state except (reportedly) Wyoming and Vermont. Most, however, live in a few major cities. The greater Miami area (Dade County)—and other parts of southern Florida—account for the largest population of Cuban Americans. New York City, Jersey City, Newark, Los Angeles, and Chicago account for a large part of the rest.

MIAMI

The Cubans in Miami have had a great influence on the city. The Hispanic community in and around Miami provides millions of dollars in purchasing power. Dade County has become a dynamic business and cultural center. Miami is officially bilingual. All public forms and documents must appear in both English and Spanish. The center of the Cuban community is "Little Havana," a three-and-a-half-mile strip of shops, businesses, and restaurants centered at S.W. Eighth and Flagler streets. A familiar sight is a group of men around card tables set up on the sidewalk, intent on a game of dominoes.

Cuban Americans engage in more serious cultural activities in Miami also. There are several publishers of Spanish-language books, magazines, and newspapers and a choice of Spanish-language radio stations and two television stations. Miami is becoming a center for Hispanic art and music. A Cuban American symphony orchestra plays classical music. And popular singers and musicians provide more up-to-date music with a Latin beat.

A game of dominoes in Miami

Carlos J. Arboleya

A SUCCESS STORY: CARLOS J. ARBOLEYA

Before 1959, Carlos Arboleya was the chief auditor and comptroller of Cuba's largest bank. When Castro took over all the banks and made them state property, Arboleya decided to leave Cuba with his wife and son. He left with only $40 in his pocket.

The family landed in Miami, and Arboleya tried to get a job in a bank. He was told he was overqualified for any of the available jobs. He decided he must take any position he could get; he was finally offered a job as a clerk in a shoe factory and he took it. "I didn't know a thing about shoes when I started," he said. A year and a half later he had become a vice president of the company. Eventually Arboleya went back to banking. In 1964 he joined the Fidelity National Bank and was later named president and chief executive officer. He was the first Cuban American to become president of a U.S. national bank. For the past fifteen years Arboleya has been vice-chairman of the Barnett Bank of South Florida.

At first, most of the Cuban refugees did not feel driven to succeed in the United States. Their attention was focused on freeing their homeland from Castro. Most Cuban Americans did not think of their stay in the United States as permanent. So very few of them bought permanent residences. The fall of Castro was expected any moment. One immigrant remembers the atmosphere in Miami during those years:

> *Cubans would gather after Sunday mass to discuss the events of the week. . . . The usual parting words were: "We'll celebrate* La Nochebuena *[Christmas Eve] in Cuba this year," or "We'll soon eat our* lechoncito asado *[traditional roast pork] in our country."*
>
> Source: Nestor Carbonell, *And the Russians Stayed: The Sovietization of Cuba.* (New York: Morrow, 1989), p. 306.

Both the Bay of Pigs invasion and the missile crisis were heavy blows to the early exile community. It had become clear that the United States was not going to war to overthrow Castro. More and more, after the mid-1960s, Cuban Americans realized that the liberation of Cuba was not realistic. Their state of mind changed from that of refugees to immigrants. This was the time when so many Cuban Americans seemed to be overachievers. They were the people who quickly learned new skills, worked extra hours at extra jobs to put themselves through school, and managed to climb the ladder of success.

The younger generation is following in their footsteps. Many of them have been born here and think more about meeting mortgage and insurance payments than they do about freeing Cuba. Even many of those who were born in Cuba

Some Cubans, such as this couple in Miami, have become prosperous in the United States.

have no desire to return. As Carlos López, Miami post office worker who fled the island in 1981, says, "Go [to Cuba] for what? To cry and see the poor people?"[1]

CUBAN AMERICAN LIFE-STYLES

Family Roles Middle-class Cuban life in the old country was centered around the family, especially around the mother. The woman's place was in the home as nurturer and companion for both husband and children. She provided a midday meal for which the husband came home, and she did not routinely accompany him on business outings.

[1]*Source: Newsweek,* March 26, 1990, p. 29.

Today in the United States, the Cuban American woman has taken on the life of the community she lives in. In Miami, it is more conservative and old-fashioned than in other American cities. While the wife may also have become a wage earner, the home and family are still central. Acculturation, or the taking up of new social patterns, has happened more slowly there, perhaps because of the size of the community and because of the relatively large number of older people. (On the one hand, the extended family continues to flourish in Miami, with the elderly taking important roles as housekeepers and baby-sitters. And on the other hand, those elderly who live alone have become a serious social and economic problem for the Cuban community.) While young girls are just beginning to be allowed to date without a chaperone (older

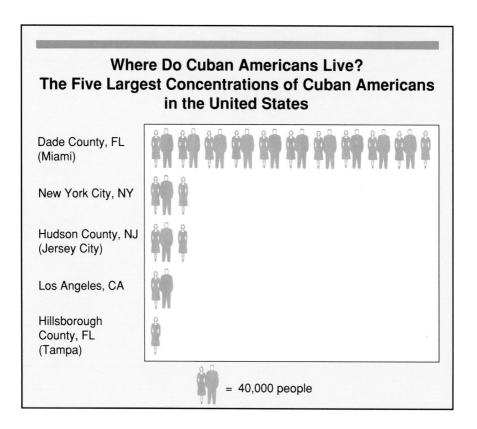

Where Do Cuban Americans Live?
The Five Largest Concentrations of Cuban Americans in the United States

Dade County, FL (Miami)

New York City, NY

Hudson County, NJ (Jersey City)

Los Angeles, CA

Hillsborough County, FL (Tampa)

= 40,000 people

companion) in Miami, in other cities they are dating, or at least double-dating, much like other Americans today.

In other cities, Cuban American women have become more separated from their Cuban life-style. The wife contributes not only equal work hours but companionship and support on an equal social level. Women are more likely to join other women in social activities apart from their husbands than they did when they were in Cuba.

Class and Education   Forty percent of all Cuban Americans live in Miami and most of them are middle class. Those who live elsewhere are less concentrated in the middle class. Though Cuban Americans tend to form compact neighborhoods everywhere, outside of South Florida they seem to adjust to their surroundings more easily.

In Miami, Cuban Americans have developed a private elementary and secondary school system, which initially was Catholic, but more recently has become more and more non-church oriented. Most Cuban American children go to public school. In 1987 over 61 percent of all Cuban Americans over the age of twenty-five had completed high school, compared to 77 percent of all whites in the United States. Some Cuban Americans go on to get college degrees, many with the aid of the Cuban Student Loan program. A number of these students become teachers and professors in colleges and universities.

In 1982, about 10 percent of all Cuban Americans earned more than $45,000 a year, and approximately 40 percent were considered poor. Many Cubans still have low incomes. In 1987 half the families earned less than $27,000. Many of the working poor are seasonal workers in services and tourism in Florida, others are agricultural workers in Florida and Louisiana, and still others in New York and New Jersey are piece workers in the garment industry and earn low wages.

Picadillo (ground beef, with olives, raisins, and pimento) served with fried plantain and rice

CUBAN AMERICAN FOOD

Cuban American specialities include many meat or chicken dishes served with rice, often flavored with saffron, pimento, and spices. Black beans are a favorite and are served with roast pork for Christmas dinner. Salt cod, or *bacalao,* is a traditional Cuban dish, as are tamales stuffed with pork or other meats. Shrimp and fish are served in all forms, and fruits, such as plantains, bananas, and guavas, are popular. *Turrón,* a sweet candy like pralines, is served at Christmastime, and *flan,* or caramel custard, is an everyday delight for dessert.

SOME CUBAN AMERICAN CELEBRATIONS

Fiesta de Quince Años The *fiesta de quince años* is a coming-of-age party for a girl when she reaches her fifteenth birthday. Unlike the "sweet sixteen" party celebrated around the United States, the Cuban American party carries somewhat more serious overtones of a rite of puberty and a preparation for marriage. Traditionally, a Cuban girl could be married at age fifteen.

Today, especially in Miami, the fiesta de quince años gives some Cuban Americans the opportunity to put on a large and lavish party and display their social position. Weddinglike, the party involves expensive dresses, elaborate gifts, and quantities of food and drink.

New Year's Eve For Cuban Americans, as for most people in the United States, New Year's Eve is a time of getting together with friends and toasting the new year with champagne and song. Cubans often substitute *sidra española,* a hard apple cider. Finally, to bring good luck, they eat twelve grapes at midnight, one for each month of the coming year.

A fiesta de quince años being celebrated in Key Biscayne, Florida

Most Cuban Americans are Roman Catholic. Many churches in the Miami area have masses in Spanish every day. They are thriving under the influx of so many new parishioners. In addition, there are a small number of Cubans, mostly blacks, who practice a cult religion called *santeria,* which is a mixture of Catholicism and African ritual.

The patron saint of Cuba is called *Nuestra Señora de la Caridad del Cobre,* or the Virgin of Cobre. In many Cuban American churches, a special celebration for her is held on September 8. Dressed in white lace, with a mantle of blue and gold, a statue of the Virgin is carried in a traditional procession throughout the church.

This is her story. In the sixteenth century, when the Spanish ruled Cuba, three men (two Indians and a freed slave) set out to sea in a boat after a bad storm. They found a board floating on the water. On the board stood a statue of the Virgin. Written on the board were the words "I am the Virgin of Charity *(Caridad)."*

The men took the board and the statue home with them and built a shrine. Over the years, as the story goes, the statue disappeared several times, and it was decided that the Virgin needed a larger shrine. Finally, a little girl saw an apparition in the Sierra Maestra near some copper *(cobre)* mines. People took this as a sign that the Virgin wanted her shrine nearby, and it was constructed there. Through the years, Cubans have brought great numbers of offerings or gifts in thanks for her blessings. In 1916, Pope Benedict named the Virgin of Cobre the patron saint of Cuba. In 1959, to celebrate Castro's revolution, people made a procession around the island with the statue of the Virgin. Afterward it was returned to the shrine in the Sierra Maestra.

Ileana Ros-Lehtinen

Republican Ileana Ros-Lehtinen was elected to the U.S. House of Representatives in 1989. She is the first Cuban American, as well as the first Hispanic woman, to be elected to Congress. She won in the special election held following the death of Claude Pepper, popular longtime congressman from the Miami district in Florida. Her margin of victory was 53 to 47 percent of the vote. Her opponent had asked people to vote for him because he was "American." The Cuban American voters replied with a resounding 90 percent of their vote for Ros-Lehtinen, though only 12 percent of the non-Cuban American voters gave her their vote. Her election shows how important the Cuban American vote has become in Florida.

Congresswoman Ros-Lehtinen was born in Havana in 1952 and is a thirty-year resident of Florida.

Jose Canseco

Jose Canseco is the highest-paid major league baseball player in the United States and earns about $4.5 million a year. He plays outfield for the Oakland Athletics. In 1986 he was voted Rookie of the Year and, in 1988, the Most Valuable Player of the Year by the Baseball Writers' Association. In the same year, he made a new baseball record and became the first member of the "40/40 Club." This means he hit forty home runs and stole forty bases in one season. So far he is the only person to have done it.

Canseco was born in 1964 in Havana. His father brought the family to Miami nine months later "because communism is a rotten thing." Jose attended Coral Park High School in southwest Miami, and was drafted by the Oakland organization in 1982. His twin brother Ozzie is also a baseball player. Cuban Americans in Miami are very proud of Canseco and have named a portion of S.W. Sixteenth Street—not far from José Martí Street—"Jose Canseco Street."

A MUSICIAN'S STORY

Adolfo Ponce   In Cuba, Ponce was a famous symphony violinist and musical director. His son, Adolfito, also a violinist, was a music student in Havana. His teachers said he was the most talented violin student in Cuba.

Ponce senior asked for and received permission to leave Cuba in 1980. His son, then fifteen years old, was refused permission. Castro usually does not allow anyone of military age (which starts at fifteen) to emigrate. Ponce left for Miami and changed careers. Since his arrival, he has built up a successful construction company.

In 1990 Adolfito carried out, with the help of his father, a long-planned escape from Cuba. He had received permission to play with a touring orchestra in Mexico and notified his father. His father flew to Puerto Vallarta and then drove to Tepic, where he hoped to see Adolfito and get him away from the Cuban officials. Made to perform in disguise, then whisked away from place to place, Adolfito was kept from his father. Finally, in a bold move, the elder Ponce grabbed the son and drove away with him. Cuban officials followed in a hair-raising car chase, but the Ponces managed to escape across the border into the United States.

Back in Miami, Adolfito went to work for his father. They started a symphony orchestra in Miami and are once again able to play music together.

A WINDSURFER'S STORY

Lester Moreno Perez   Seventeen-year-old Lester Moreno Perez did the "impossible." He fled Cuba on a sailboard. With a little help, he made it to Florida.

At 8:30 on the night of March 1, 1990, Moreno Perez inched his way along a beach on the north coast of Cuba. When he was sure that no one was looking, he carefully slid his sailboard into the water. He stepped onto it and grabbed the boom with both hands.

Moreno Perez knew there were sharks in these waters, but he tried not to think about it. He said later:

 *Ever since I left, I could see the sharks coming out and in, coming up on the board. I was hoping and thinking they were dolphins, but when the sun came up, I could see there was no way they were dolphins.*

Source: As quoted in "Board Sailor," *Sports Illustrated*, April 23, 1990, p. 70.

Moreno Perez sailed all night. Then the boom that held his sail broke and he began to drift. Luckily for him, he was spotted by a freighter and taken aboard—just thirty miles south of Key West. His feet were covered with sores from the sailboard's foot straps, and his hands were a mass of blisters. But he had survived ten hours and sixty miles on the open water and had made his way to freedom. That was the main thing.

Lester Moreno Perez

Events in Eastern Europe One after another, in 1989 the Communist countries broke away from the Soviet bloc and demanded new elections and democratic forms of government. Almost overnight, it seemed, forty years of oppressive rule was ended. The Berlin Wall was torn down, and East Germany asked for a Western-style government. In Poland, the antigovernment Solidarity movement came to power, and in Romania and Hungary, the Communist leaders were ousted.

Many of these events had been encouraged by the new *glasnost* ("openness") policy of President Mikhail Gorbachev in the Soviet Union. In trying to reach new understanding with the West, and to salvage his deteriorating economy, he allowed the promise of new freedom and understanding to get the upper hand. It even seemed possible that the Soviet Union would break up into a number of separate countries. Everywhere in Europe, communism was in full retreat and free-market economies were spreading.

What Will the Future Bring? In the aftermath of these events, Cuban Americans especially are wondering about the future of Communist Cuba. Will Castro be able to survive if Soviet economic aid disappears? Will the excesses of his regime—suppression of the free press, lack of free elections, internal spying, imprisonment of political opponents, lack of a penal code and the right to a private lawyer, disorganization of economic life—bring about Castro's downfall?

Opinions differ. "In a free Cuban election Fidel Castro would receive less than ten percent of the votes," wrote one observer.[1]

[1]*Source:* Jacobo Timerman, "Reflections: A Summer in the Revolution: 1987," *New Yorker,* August 13, 1990, p. 72.

Others remain more skeptical. Castro is still an able and powerful figure, who seems to have absolute control of his people. Many believe most Cubans are better off than they have ever been, with better health care and education. And despite signs of Soviet disaffection with Cuba, Castro remains publicly committed to a socialist future and the Communist Party.

> *Fidel has outlasted seven U.S. presidents and five Soviet leaders. He has been in power longer than any world figure except King Hussein of Jordan, and he could well be Cuba's leader for another twenty years.*
>
> Source: Peter G. Bourne, *Fidel: A Biography of Fidel Castro* (New York: Dodd, Mead, 1986), p. 305.

However, while some exiles long to return to Cuba, a poll taken by station WLTV in Miami reported that only one in five Cubans would return. No one can say for sure what will happen, but it is important to remember that many Cuban Americans have made new and successful lives in the United States. Many children have been born to them since 1959, and the young people, especially, know nothing of the pre-Castro days in Cuba. A Marielito has put it succinctly:

> *Those who came before us still think that they will find a way to go back. To do it they would have to travel through time, not just get in a boat. There is no pre-Castro Cuba any more. Cuba is his, just as Fidel says. . . .*
>
> Source: As quoted in David Rieff, *Going to Miami: Exiles, Tourists, and Refugees in the New America* (Boston: Little, Brown, 1987), p. 207.

José Martí parade in Miami

Sources

Books

Boone, Margaret S. *Capital Cubans: Refugee Adaptation in Washington, D.C.* New York: AMS Press, 1989.

Bourne, Peter G. *Fidel: A Biography of Fidel Castro.* New York: Dodd, Mead, 1986.

Carbonell, Nestor. *And the Russians Stayed: The Sovietization of Cuba.* New York: Morrow, 1989.

Curtin, Philip D. *The Atlantic Slave Trade: A Census.* Madison: Univ. of Wisconsin Press, 1969.

Daniels, Roger. *Coming to America: A History of Immigration and Ethnicity in American Life.* New York: HarperCollins, 1990.

Dolan, Jay P. *The Immigrant Church, Irish and German Catholics, 1818–1865.* Baltimore: Johns Hopkins Univ. Press, 1975.

Encinosa, Enrique. *Cuba: The Unfinished Revolution.* Austin, Tex.: Eakin Publications, 1988.

Garver, Susan, and Paula McGuire. *Coming to North America from Mexico, Cuba, and Puerto Rico.* New York: Delacorte, 1981.

Harvard Encyclopedia of Ethnic Groups. Cambridge: Harvard Univ. Press, 1980.

Portes, Alejandro, and Robert L. Bach. *Latin Journey: Cuban and Mexican Immigrants in the U.S.* Berkeley: Univ. of California Press, 1985.

Reimers, David. *Still the Golden Door: The Third World Comes to America, 1943–1983.* New York: Columbia Univ. Press, 1985.

Rieff, David. *Going to Miami: Exiles, Tourists, and Refugees in the New America.* Boston: Little, Brown, 1987.

Periodicals

"The Battle with Himself." *Gentleman's Quarterly,* May 1989, p. 24.

"Board Sailor." *Sports Illustrated,* April 23, 1990, pp. 68–70.

"Florida Waits for Fidel to Fall." *Newsweek,* March 26, 1990.

"Midnight Race for Freedom." *Reader's Digest,* September 1989, pp. 198–204.

"The Revolution at 30." *Newsweek,* January 9, 1989, pp. 36–37.

Index